For Your Garden

GARDEN ANTIQUES AND COLLECTIBLES

For Your Garden

GARDEN ANTIQUES AND COLLECTIBLES

Teri Dunn

FRIEDMAN/FAIRFAX
PUBLISHERS

DEDICATION

For Ted Putnam (fellow horticulturist) and Milissa Putnam (finder of treasures).

A FRIEDMAN/FAIRFAX BOOK
Please visit our website: www.metrobooks.com

© 2000, 1999 by Michael Friedman Publishing Group, Inc.

Library of Congress Cataloging-in-Publication Data available upon request.

ISBN 1-56799-785-6

Editor: Susan Lauzau
Art Director: Jeff Batzli
Designer: Jennifer Markson
Photography Editor: Wendy Missan
Production Manager: Richela Fabian

Color separations by Fine Arts Repro House Co., Ltd.
Printed in China by Midas Printing Limited

3 5 7 9 10 8 6 4 2

Distributed by Sterling Publishing Company, Inc.
387 Park Avenue South
New York, NY 10016
Distributed in Canada by Sterling Publishing
Canadian Manda Group
One Atlantic Avenue, Suite 105
Toronto, Ontario, Canada M6K 3E7
Distributed in Australia by
Capricorn Link (Australia) Pty Ltd.
P.O. Box 6651
Baulkham Hills, Business Centre, NSW 2153, Australia

Table of Contents

INTRODUCTION

The appeal of antiques in a garden is obvious: embellishments of a certain age give the space an irresistible sense of having been comfortably in place for a long time. Vintage garden ornaments and collectibles are especially helpful in a young or freshly redone garden, where you may be impatient for your plants to mature and spread out or where you long for a sense of peaceful retreat. A time-worn statue, weathered urn, old-fashioned seat, or retired cart, carefully situated, grants the garden the air of permanence you seek—with style.

When a garden accent looks as if it has settled into its spot over time, count the idea a success. Moss or lichens embracing a statue and ivy twining around an old birdbath or armillary sphere bestow a mellowing effect. An air of stability and grace settles over the garden.

Trendy catalogs, garden accessory shops, and cluttered flea markets abound with chances for you to acquire authentic antiques or good reproductions, from highly formal or contrived pieces to ones that exude rustic or whimsical charm. But buyer beware: a high price tag doesn't guarantee authenticity.

Vintage ornaments are gaining in popularity, so if you hope to have a few, you'd do wise to start looking now. Pieces from European manors or the estates of the Old South can fetch thousands of dollars; others, like 1950s metal furniture, are currently quite trendy and sure to rise in price. If you do acquire something expensive, or are lucky enough to receive an heirloom or another item that has sentimental value, be sure to site it with care and secure it in place if you can. There's actually a small but growing subculture of garden bandits who know or suspect the value of that which they purloin.

In the end, the beauty of introducing "old" treasures to your garden is the fact that they do more than create an enchanting vignette or enhance the mood. They combine an enduring piece of man-made art with the ageless beauty of nature, enriching the garden for you as well as for admiring visitors.

ABOVE: Since the gate is the portal to the garden, and is often responsible for visitors' first impressions, you might invest in an old gate to give your garden that desirable feeling of being well-established. Check flea markets, estate sales, architectural salvage yards, and large rural junk shops for vintage examples. You may have to repair or replace hardware or latches, but the impact the gate brings to the garden will be well worth the trouble.

OPPOSITE: Nestled into an overgrown corner and joined by a putto—a figure of an infant boy, popular in Renaissance art—this retired porcelain bathtub gains new cachet as a garden ornament. The angled juxtaposition of the rustic bench in the foreground grants the pair a little privacy, lending the scene a sense of retreat from the busy world.

ABOVE: Herb plants, thanks to their naturally exuberant growth habits, look splendid in the company of rustic garden ornaments. Here, a retired garden cultivator fits the bill perfectly—its rusty metal and weatherbeaten wood are right at home in the garden's informal lushness.

OPPOSITE: Full sun, high summer, the heady fragrance of blooming lavender—it's the perfect setting for a sundial. If you can't find a sundial with a pedestal high enough or grand enough, shop for one separately or have a metal shop fashion a sturdy base for you. Just be sure the sundial plate itself is securely attached and, of course, level, should you intend to read it.

LEFT: Without inviting seats nearby, some of your favorite flower displays may be swiftly bypassed by garden visitors. This pair of august seats conveys permanence and a sense that the garden is well-established even when the surrounding plants are not particularly old or imposing—an impression desired by most gardeners. The benches promise the supreme respite, an opportunity to compose oneself in a quiet, semishady corner.

OPPOSITE: Lead or stone "baskets of fruit" are sometimes seen in historic European estates; their suggestion of a generous, bountiful harvest make them a natural for placement in the heart of the garden. This modern replica stands up to the elements and weighs less, which makes it a pleasing alternative to an authentic piece, especially if you find the original antiques cost-prohibitive or difficult to find. In either case, because these designs are inevitably a bit top-heavy, make certain to position the pieces securely on the ground.

ABOVE: An old, carved door and handmade storage jars and jugs in various sizes create a scene-stealing composition. The saturated blue paint, rubbed through to unfinished wood in places, is a pleasing counterpoint to the neutral, earthy shades of the vessels. This type of grouping is well worth re-creating, particularly if you haven't the time or inclination to fill every corner with plants yet you want great drama.

RIGHT: Fresh paint brings a sense of exuberance to otherwise staid old patio chairs, without sacrificing their original form. The rich cobalt blue used here doesn't shout out its presence, yet it provides welcome contrast to the frothy white and bold crimson blooms in the urn.

ABOVE: This beautiful old clay pot, liberally planted with bright blooms, gains additional character when a small carved statue is placed next to it. Though of different materials and construction (one formed by the potter's hand, the other by the carver's knife), the combination works because of their folksy character, and because neither piece is new. They are like two old friends that have weathered the years together, and have settled into the garden to stay.

OPPOSITE: Tuck an aged, empty oil jar into a corner of your perennial bed and enjoy the many facets it brings to the garden. The soft, warm umber color seems to go with any flower color, while the size and shape contribute ample contrast in form. Tipped on its side, the vessel appears long forgotten, perhaps discarded by some ancient civilization. Certainly, without this magnificent jar, the same spot would be far less intriguing.

LEFT: In the grand old British garden of Hampton Court, a fountain composed of an antique keystone and a weathered basin bring repose in the long shadows of late afternoon. Here both the style and age of the display confer a wonderful, ageless tranquility.

ABOVE: In an area where plantings are uncomplicated, dare to place a more elaborate seat, such as this venerable old beauty at Washington D.C.'s famed Dumbarton Oaks. The obvious age and classical lines of this piece give the setting real elegance.

ABOVE: Pieces made of copper and bronze, or alloys thereof, typically gain a handsome green patina as they age. Nor does this process take decades; in fact, several winters out in the garden in a cool or rainy climate ought to do the trick. Alternatively, some suppliers sell pieces that already have this timeworn look.

OPPOSITE: A touch of whimsy is always welcome, and it needn't be on ground level among the plants. Birds may or may not actually use these grand old quarters, but you can be sure that human garden visitors will be instantly drawn to the spot and will enjoy the sense of history it suggests with such unabashed charm.

Chapter One

GARDEN ORNAMENT

*T*he best garden ornaments are those that simply strike your fancy. Deliberately or unwittingly, you are likely to choose something that "fits" with your taste in garden plants, making placement less challenging than you might originally suspect when you are shopping, out of sight of your yard. You may prefer graceful scenes with demure statues, or perhaps you like bolder, more dramatic statements made with a formal sundial or birdbath situated in the center of a flower bed. There is a vast range of styles from which you might choose, and certainly an appropriate antique or funky collectible can be found to suit every garden.

A word to the wise: as you shop, be wary of ornaments that display names or dates, as they may have been purloined from an estate or old cemetery. Rough edges that suggest a piece was chipped off a pedestal or wall are further cues that you may be looking at "hot" merchandise. For big-ticket items, insist on documentation of origin and composition, and get a receipt.

By its very nature, a garden is in a constant state of change, through the seasons and over the years. Well-chosen ornaments impart a sense of constancy in the midst of this constant flux, conferring a welcome feeling of age and stability. Leaves and flowers may burgeon all around a piece, or gradually insinuate themselves into its base and crevices, but the aged ornament will stand firm and serene as its world grows around it.

ABOVE: The pairing of a venerable ram's head sculpture (which probably originated in Mexico or South America) and small, jaunty daffodils is a stirring juxtaposition of antiquity and fresh, new life.

OPPOSITE: Elegantly formed statues of gods or goddesses are ideal for formal settings. Savvy placement will make a statue a garden focal point, granting weight and character to an otherwise undistinguished spot. Secure anchoring is critical, though, and shelter offered by nearby plants is wise, as such pieces can otherwise topple in stormy weather.

ABOVE: The graceful lines of the girl's body have been worn and smoothed by rain, wind, and sun, as has her offered seashell birdbath, yet the little birds still return year after year. A clearing in a quiet woodland garden is the perfect setting for the contemplative patience of this weatherbeaten figure.

OPPOSITE: In the legend, the inscrutable Sphinx (with the body of a lion, wings of a bird, and head of a woman) held its ground for many years while passersby tried and failed to answer its riddles. A modern replica ought to be placed along a path or wall, then, in a location where encroaching plants and the weather will eventually mute but never completely hide its mysterious demeanor.

ABOVE LEFT: Symbolic sculptures such as this Buddha figure are much more than mere decoration. They may be seen to soothe, bless, and protect their surroundings as well as those visitors who stop to ponder them. Plus, the older the piece, the more sincere or imposing the deity's presence seems.

ABOVE RIGHT: Mythological creatures such as this diminutive stone heraldic beast (note the coat of arms beneath its paws) are intriguing images in the garden. Situated in the midst of a fern bed and firmly anchored to a stone urn filled with water, this fellow looks like he is quietly guarding the scene.

OPPOSITE: The delicate beauty of pink azalea blossoms are a sure match for a Japanese-style stone lantern. Because this lantern's edges are worn and its surface is blanketed with velvety moss, a beguiling impression of antiquity reigns. A brand new ornament or one with a polished surface would miss completely the opportunity to foster this air of steadfastness and strength.

ABOVE: Shrubs are the foundation of almost every garden plan, and shrubby plants such as this ceanothus (or California lilac, as it is sometimes known) call for strong ornament that help anchor the scene. Heroic and mythological figures are naturally imposing and can stand up to the company of handsome, substantial plants. Where a statue won't fit, consider a large plaque, securely mounted on a support such as a wall or fence.

RIGHT: When you mount panels of ornamental tiles or a splendid architectural fragment over a garden fence or entrance, the eye is inevitably drawn upward. Flesh-and-blood people and whimsical terra-cotta characters both seem to pause and regard one another. Visitors to this garden will undoubtedly emerge with the pleasant sensation that they have been pilgrims traveling in a timeless world.

OPPOSITE: A stone arch requiring a gate is much better served by a panel of cast iron than by more vulnerable wood. The iron is a stronger, more imposing partner to the massive arch, and lends a prestigious air to the gateway. In addition, the scrolled iron bars permit a tempting peek into the garden, a treat not possible with a more solidly constructed door.

RIGHT: If you are the sort of gardener who allows plants and creatures in your garden—both the planned ones and the uninvited ones—to go their own way, you may be inclined to incorporate elaborate garden ornaments with interesting lines and features. Here, a decorative iron gate creates a vivid scene when a spider and the prickly red stem of a raspberry cane are given free rein.

ABOVE LEFT: Simplicity rules in this modest sundial display, whose elegant lines are all the more obvious in a garden's off-season. Note how the pedestal's sandy hue exudes a natural warmth that cast concrete never can.

ABOVE RIGHT: This armillary sphere, with its contrived arrow and supporting figure, is of supremely exuberant design. A piece like this is most at home in an informal setting, where its mood of motion will consort well with lively blossoms and foliage tossing in the breeze.

OPPOSITE: What kind of ornament can you place in the company of topiary or spiky perennials such as these foxgloves? It needs to be somewhat formal, and must answer to the timelessness of the shrubs as well as the fleeting beauty of the flowers—a sundial on a modest pedestal is the beautiful solution. In addition, the aged green patina of the dial's surface blends well with the color scheme of this stately garden.

ABOVE: Birdbaths come in a tremendous range of sizes, shapes, styles, and colors. Yours will fit in best if you take care to choose one that is not too large for its surroundings. Older pieces may be worn, chipped, or even cracked, so perform any patching or repair work before placing it in the garden and adding water.

OPPOSITE: The unassuming balustrade design of this birdbath pedestal hints that it was once part of a greater display along a grand porch or balcony. How aptly that feel works with a garden of young perennials still filling in their allotted areas—not to mention the single sculpted bird, just waiting to be joined by a host of feathered companions.

ABOVE LEFT: Foliage plants are rarely garden standouts on their own, but add a sculpture to the bed, and the area gains fresh interest. The angel's quiet gaze as well as its chalky, hard surface call attention to the contrasting glossy texture and lush growth that envelops it.

ABOVE RIGHT: A weeping cherry tree is the perfect spot to nestle in a little garden sculpture. The mood is a bit wistful; the cherry petals will fall, and the adjacent spring-flowering bulbs will fade, but the little boy's sweet illusion of agelessness will linger at the spot.

RIGHT: He never grows older, and the water never stops flowing—this small, "antiqued" fountain statue of a little boy at the pond's edge creates an eternal and charming presence. This is a modern replica of a well-loved design, so the fountain is guaranteed to be in good working order. If you invest in an antique fountain, you will probably need to have the plumbing updated to ensure a generous flow of water.

Chapter Two

ANTIQUE AND VINTAGE FURNITURE

A seat in the garden is always inviting—a weathered bench or an intriguing antique chair has an irresistible, almost haunting appeal. Maybe that is because old chairs, benches, and accompanying tables hint at other visitors before you who have paused and rested.

Indeed, garden furnishings, above all other ornaments, beckon to guests, enticing them to view and savor the scene from a different angle. Garden seats provide them with an opportunity to see in a completely new way while relaxing, not standing and stopping, not strolling. Seats invite visitors to participate, to get down on the garden's level.

And as simple decor, garden furniture has the virtue of exuding an aura of leisure. It evokes slow afternoons that drift into quiet evenings of deepening shadows, of long, golden summers and snow-cushioned winters, of years and generations that come and go.

No wonder then, that choosing garden furniture is such a personal and visceral decision. Shop with an open mind and heart. Touch a seat, run your hand over its surfaces, picture it in a secluded corner of your garden or on your patio or deck. Sit down, breath deeply, and imagine yourself enfolded comfortably in its confines.

When you get the chair home, put it to use immediately. Later, you can brush off rust or dirt residue, install braces, add fresh paint and bright cushions, and decorate the environs with twining plants, nearby pots of herbs, and a tall glass of iced juice. Today, all you need to know is that an old friend has arrived.

OPPOSITE: An artifact of grand old parks and estates, the "tree seat" is designed in interlocking sections to fit around the trunk of a large shade tree. If you are lucky enough to find a full set, the charming old seat will immediately confer a feeling of stateliness to the largest tree on your lawn (even if the tree still has more growing to do).

RIGHT: Conversation, confidences, old stories—this informal set of vintage chairs and small table promises moments or hours of comfortable companionship. A metal plant stand painted to match offers a charming and appropriate accompaniment to the set, and provides an ideal resting place for plants, unused pots, and any other ornaments the gardener might fancy.

LEFT: The play of light and shadow is never more soothing than when it is dancing on the surface of something old and treasured. Carved wooden benches are indeed cherished pieces; if you cannot find one that is intact or in sufficiently good condition for use, you may be able, with care, to graft a decorative back onto a newer seat.

OPPOSITE: The artistic lines and intricate detailing on a weathered stone bench invite you to pause and marvel at its obvious age. The encroaching pink phlox link the bench to the garden successfully, but cannot steal the show from the grand old seat.

ABOVE: Embraced by abundant wildflowers, this nearly hidden cast-iron bench beckons silently, promising a spot for quiet repose. A secluded corner is an ideal setting for a vintage bench—allowing the garden to grow up around it only enhances the feeling of privacy. Indulge enthusiastic growers somewhat, but note that you'll almost certainly need to trim back overhanging plants after a time.

OPPOSITE: Matching garden furniture to adjacent plants is an art that requires a good eye and a healthy dose of creativity—this juxtaposition of an antique cast-iron English bench with the classically handsome spires of acanthus is a resounding success. The plant's broad, oversized leaves balance the intense verticality of the flower stalks, and both provide an interesting counterpoint in texture and form to the Gothic-inspired bench.

ABOVE LEFT: Refresh an old patio chair with coat of paint every now and then (be sure to use a paint specially formulated for exterior use). Not only does the piece last longer, you get a new chance to create appealing color combinations in the yard.

ABOVE RIGHT: Elaborate and well-crafted caning is a fading art, so if you find such a chair, grab it, bring it home, and see what can be done to repair it if need be. Because it is vulnerable to wet weather, place the caned chair under shelter (which will also give the sitter appreciated shade) and bring it indoors when necessary. Such chairs are lovely garden accents because they are made of natural materials and have a gentle, weathered color that blends well with flowers and foliage, particularly in informal or cottage-style gardens.

OPPOSITE: A hanging seat is an unorthodox choice, and plain wicker is an unconventional material for outdoor exposure, yet this seat, reminiscent of a sheltering cocoon or a protective eggshell, offers a haven that is virtually irresistible. Set in a peaceful woodland garden, off the path and beside a rushing stream, this rather eccentric hanging chair is sure to be a favorite of those garden visitors looking for a break from the busy world.

ABOVE: Off-season's hush invites flights of fancy—an old-fashioned iron bench and chairs conjure images of a lazy summer day, perhaps with finely dressed Victorian ladies and gentlemen perched on the seats.

RIGHT: This lonely, snow-covered bench waits under an arbor for spring to return. A more modern or trendy seat would lack the venerable heft and patient demeanor of this classic old one. In spring and summer, the climbers that swathe the arbor create a shady, secluded retreat.

ABOVE: They don't build them like they used to: this stylish variation on the classic Adirondack chair is the definition of outdoor-seating comfort. A slightly tilted back and deep, contoured seat urge you to stay, and wide arms can support a cool drink, a paperback book, and your languid arms. Cedar or redwood chairs last for many years.

LEFT: Ah, the alluring "courting swing." In keeping with its old-fashioned function, you'd do wise to invest in a vintage one. If an old one isn't available, give a newer one a fetching antiqued look with a coat of soft-hued paint.

ABOVE: Placed in the midst of thick-growing Matilija poppy foliage and overhung by abundant white lilies, this sweetheart cafe chair imparts a touch of whimsy to the corner of this city garden. Note the way the color of the chair brings out the blue tones in the potted agave nearby. Take a cue from this setting, and choose the colors of garden ornaments and plants to complement or accent one another.

Chapter Three

WHIMSICAL TOUCHES

Adding ornament to a garden should be fun—the process itself should be as engaging as the final result. Perhaps you know exactly what you want—a ship's lantern or an old wheelbarrow that you will fill with annuals—and you are fortunate enough to find it. But go hunting with an open mind anyway. You will be pleasantly surprised at the nifty things you find and at the offbeat uses to which you can put familiar objects.

Maybe you have a particular spot in mind for the antique tool, funky birdhouse, or little statue you are searching for. Or perhaps (as is so often the case with an impulsive plant purchase) you'll find an item you can't resist, then return home undecided about its place in your garden. Indeed, half the fun of such spontaneous purchases is the inevitable walk around the yard with the object in your hand, as you ponder where to put it.

Also consider an object's weather-worthiness. Those that were already outdoor residents, like wheels or heavy pots, can become permanent fixtures. But others—an attractive watering can, for instance—may have to assume their positions in milder weather and be removed to storage in the off-season.

The attraction of whimsical ornaments is that they give your garden its own special personality. Decorating your garden with fanciful objects is an act of playfulness and joy. From start to finish, it gives your gardening experience an extra dimension of adventure.

ABOVE: Some watering cans may be too ancient or too lovely to actually use, but they make enchanting garden ornaments. Utility—even if faded—is always beautiful in its own right. Set an unusual vintage can on a bench, atop a garden wall, or on a wide stairstep for a charming, natural-looking tableau.

OPPOSITE: Give some thought to color combinations when you include antique decor in your garden. Weathered wooden artifacts gain enchanting warmth in the company of red and bronze leaves and flowers.

ABOVE LEFT: An old galvanized metal watering can, complete with an imposing, hand-punched rose, looks right at home at the edge of a flower bed, as if the gardener was just taking a break and will be back shortly. When something this useful becomes decor, you suddenly realize how handsomely designed it is.

ABOVE RIGHT: Old machinery sometimes makes for whimsical garden decor. Oftentimes, the objects were sturdily built (thus ought to be able to weather outdoor conditions) and had attractive details that make them a handsome addition. They can also be conversation pieces, as your friends speculate what they were used for; this item, photographed in an English garden, is a "mangle," which squeezed excess water from laundered clothing and sheets.

OPPOSITE: If you can find one, an old millstone makes a wonderful garden ornament—once you lug it into position, that is, as they can be extremely heavy and unwieldy. Some gardeners convert the stone into a simple bubbling fountain.

ABOVE: Everything about this vintage fountain suggests languor and tranquility. The sunlight plays off the water's surface, moss blankets the crevices and edges, and the water bubbles and drips rather than making the big, dramatic splashes often associated with modern or formal fountains.

OPPOSITE: When you go shopping for fountains, you'll discover that the options are endless. Many are sleek and modern, but consider something old and full of character, like this theatrical elephant. His presence in a simple, shallow pool conjures evocative images of far-off lands.

LEFT: A creative landscaper saw an interesting opportunity in the arching shape and cross slats of a retired dory. Part of the prow is buried for stability, and a climbing vine has successfully been trained up the sides, integrating this whimsical item more firmly into the garden.

RIGHT: Birdhouses are a cottage industry; you can buy adorable ones from gardening catalogs, pick up rustic ones from roadside hobbyists, stumble across neglected ones in barn sales, or even make your own from salvaged materials. Even if birds never take up residence, a birdhouse in the garden offers pleasure enough with its diminutive charm.

ABOVE: Gazing balls have gone in and out of style. Advocates rhapsodize about the mirrored reflections of clouds, branches, foliage, and blossoms. The availability of quieter colors, such as this deep blue one, and non-traditional mounts and pedestals also argue for a fresh appraisal. The fact is, the presence of a thoughtfully placed gazing ball can be downright fanciful.

ABOVE: The ornamental wheelbarrow, here nearly overrrun with a rambling rose, is an idea perhaps inadvertently invented by a busy gardener who forgot to finish a planting job. A discarded wheelbarrow from a junk yard or garage sale will do the trick; you can skip the repairs if it is going to be permanently parked. You should, however, make some arrangement for drainage if none exists, so water doesn't pool around the roots after you water the plants.

ABOVE: A handcrafted ceramic jug, no longer in mint condition but certainly still useful and good-looking, occupies a secluded corner. The worn finish and old-fashioned spigot give it an appeal that makes you forget all about going to the hose.

ABOVE: Well-chosen ornaments bring immediate charm to an otherwise nondescript corner of the garden. Here, a restored lantern and stand are a beacon of interest. Its creamy slate color is different enough to be visible in the shade and against the green foliage, but complementary enough to blend in. Terra-cotta pots (one is a salvaged chimney pot) and a wire basket filled with rivers stones also add to the palette.

ABOVE: It's not a wheelbarrow—and closer inspection will surprise and delight visitors to the garden. The wheeled base came from an old baby carriage and the container is a washtub that happens to fit. The load of bountiful herbs and soil anchors it in place.

Chapter Four

POTS AND CONTAINERS

Exhibit directors at art galleries and museums say that the frame is as much a work of art as the painting within. This is not always true, but perhaps there are times when it should be. Certainly, some thought and creativity should go into the pairing.

So it is with containers and plants—a fabulous, interesting pot or planter does much for the plants it bears. The pot presents, it frames, it flatters, increasing the significance of the plants it holds. An inspired combination of plant and planter elevates the garden it adorns.

Vintage containers are much in demand, which is understandable. Prowl flea markets, yard sales, and country auctions for interesting pieces that might be put to a new use. Like other garden antiques, old containers can be assumed to be durable. They'll show the effects of weather and water and wear over the years, but therein lies their special appeal. Who can resist the grand sense of history you get from a handsome old pot? Maybe it evokes a stately British mood, maybe a classic Mediterranean feel, or maybe even a period and a place much more ancient than that.

OPPOSITE: A bloom-drenched climbing rose drapes itself over an aged Pyrenean olive oil jar, conjuring up visions of ancient secret gardens, with olive orchards beyond their walls and solitude and rich fragrances within. Remember that you needn't fill a pot with plants to make it a part of the garden; often, a beautiful pot may stand alone as an art object and be viewed like a sculpture.

RIGHT: Terra-cotta pots planted with succulents are always attractive, but this display becomes especially captivating thanks to the imaginative use of an old washstand—something that might be had for a song at a junk shop. You might need to do a bit of repair or add some new parts, but resist the urge to clean up too much—a vintage item derives its charm from the very fact that it shows its age.

ABOVE LEFT: What to plant in a rustic, aged stone container? This gardener went for texture and color, matching the rough stone surface with the heavily marked leaves of Rex begonias. The result is a pairing that makes both partners look grander.

ABOVE RIGHT: Succulents, possibly more than any other plants, look at home in older pottery. Here, burgeoning echeveria inhabits a small planter; the glazed vessel and ornament alongside underline the feeling of antiquity as well as provide harmonizing color.

OPPOSITE: Stone basins with formal, still-sharp lines deserve regal placement and careful attention to plantings, both within and nearby. Equally important is taking into account the color of the stone. Maroon, green, and white flowers and foliage bring genuine elegance to this planter's cool, pearly hue. As in a traditional border, the low-growing plants are placed in the foreground, with taller varieties occupying the back—adapt the rules of design for your containers, keeping in mind their scale and the angles from which they'll be viewed.

ABOVE: These elegant tulips look stunning because the pot is so perfect. Note that it is about as deep as the flowers are tall, providing a sense of balance. And observe how the weathered, dampened cast cement, with its silvery hues, highlights the sparkle in the creamy-hued blooms above. The pot's color is neutral enough to blend into the surrounding vegetation, too. Indeed, this deceptively plain pot truly succeeds in achieving the coveted "always been there" look.

ABOVE: Stone looks just right in the corner of a small, formal garden. A more modern pot, of plastic or clay, would look somehow insubstantial or out of step with the stone terrace. Instead, the ornamental cast-stone pot blends effortlessly with the terrace floor and the accompanying bench. The container also acts as a nicely understated supporting player to the crisp red blossoms and two tones of foliage above, enhancing rather than clashing with the plant selection.

ABOVE: Here's an idea well worth borrowing. An ornate stone planter box elevated on two stone supports (which match, but really needn't) brings its charms closer to passersby. It is also easier to water and tend the plants. Had the planter been situated on the ground, it still would have been admirable, but the delightful pedestals truly raise the container to a new level.

ABOVE: Urns of metal, especially cast iron, are widely available. Because they don't fade or crumble, they have a commanding air—they speak of endurance in a changing setting. Classic urns bring various associations to mind, and these impressions can be encouraged by judicious siting; this is the sort of pot you might unearth in an overgrown New Orleans courtyard, a rambling English estate, or an otherwise modest upstate New York shade garden.

ABOVE: Copper is a soft and beautiful metal that ages gracefully; anyone who has containers made of it longs for the aqua patina, or verdigris, that appears over time. Get creative and incorporate the venerable color into your landscape. This pot has been daringly paired with chartreuse-hued *Euphorbia palustris.*

ABOVE: When moss coats a clay pot, your garden gains a wonderful sense of history. A well-used container inevitably achieves this look with prolonged exposure to moisture within and without, but you can speed the process along on a new clay pot by keeping it in a humid place (such as a greenhouse or bathroom) for a while or by spraying a solution of buttermilk on the dampened pot surface.

ABOVE: Jaunty cosmos and bright yellow dahlias fill this metal milk pail, adding extra color to the flower garden. Adorn picnic tables, porch railings, or quiet corners of the patio with jubilant arrangements in old-fashioned country pails or vintage water buckets, bringing the bounty of the garden to the areas where people are most likely to congregate.

RIGHT: Fun and intrigue abound in this whimsical Santa Fe garden, where painted walls and window frames consort with exuberant flowers and what appears to be a very old pot. Its uneven rim and shape indicate that it was hand-thrown and shaped rather than machine-turned; handmade pots, old or new, always have this distinctive feel, so be sure to seek them out when you go container shopping.

ABOVE: A worn but lovely bas-relief decorates this small lead planter; the gardener wisely planted for minimal foliage spilling over the sides, then set it away from other pots and plants so its beauty could be appreciated from all angles. The wide, shallow form is also a bit unusual, and looks well with the taller pots that decorate the background.

LEFT: Lions' heads and garlands ring this massive stone urn. When you find a planter in excellent condition, it is imperative that you site it so that its features are not hidden. Thus boxwood, a nontrailing plant, inhabits the pot proper, and the entire thing is situated in the open and elevated above the billowing perennials.

OPPOSITE: Lead containers are rare these days for various reasons, including their heavy weight. But if you happen upon one that you like and haul it home, be sure to choose a spot for it that seems permanent. This planter is shaped specifically for a corner, where it can settle out of the way and be decorated with waves of bright flowers.